How To Live
A Christian Life

For Ron and Loraine Hodel

How To Live
A Christian Life

FROM MARTIN LUTHER'S
ON CHRISTIAN FREEDOM

Revised & Expanded
2nd Edition

Adapted by
Paul Strawn

Lutheran Press
Minneapolis

Lutheran Press, Minneapolis 55449
© 2003, 2006 by Lutheran Press
All rights reserved.
Printed in the United States of America.

2nd Edition

ISBN: 0-9748529-3-7
ISBN-13:   978-0-9748529-3-5

Library of Congress Control Number: 2006930126

Book design by Scott Krieger.
Cover art by Maria Ahrndt.

TABLE OF CONTENTS

FOREWORD

Christian bookstores nowadays are full of books written about the Christian life. Such books try to explain how to "live like a Christian" by answering questions such as: How can I increase my faith? How can I live my life in the world as a Christian? How can I be a Christian employee? How can I know God's will for my life? How can I have a Christian marriage? How can I love my spouse? How can I raise my children to be Christians? How can I talk to people who are not Christians? How can I have true inner peace? All of these questions are certainly important and are asked by those who, having come to faith in Jesus Christ, basically wonder: Now what?

In the short work that follows, the great Reformer Martin Luther answers this "Now what?" by heading to the writings of Apostle Paul and pointing out that the Christian, having come to faith in Christ, is a lot like Jesus Christ Himself. As Christ has two natures, a divine and human, so too the Christian has two natures: An old and a new. It is because of this situation that a Christian can frequently have a hard time answering the multitude of questions posed above. The old nature of the Christian constantly tugs at the new and the result can frequently be nothing but confusion. What is to be done?

Luther sorts out this mess by taking two seemingly contradictory statements from the Apostle Paul and in the process of harmonizing them, not only answers the basic question of "Now what?", but also helps to explain how the basic aspects of the life of the Christian (the Bible, the 10 Commandments, the Gospel, faith, love, good works, pastors, sermons, church services) can all be clearly and simply understood. In so doing, Luther constructs a small Christian dogmatics of sorts, and describes the essence of the Christian life.

1

CHRISTIAN FAITH

Many people think Christian faith is no more than a good attitude. Such people haven't really experienced Christian faith. They don't know how it works.

No one can write about Christian faith or know if others have written correctly about it unless he himself has been comforted by it. Whoever has been comforted by Christian faith in even the smallest way cannot cease to write, speak, think, or hear about it! This is why Christ calls faith "a spring of water welling up to eternal life"(John 4:14).

Admittedly my faith is weak. I've been tormented by

many temptations. Even with such a weak faith, however, I will try to write something about it. If what follows is not well written, I hope it is easy to understand.

The faith of a Christian can be summarized with two statements:

A Christian is the most liberated master of everyone, and subject to no one.

A Christian is the most dutiful servant of everyone, and subject to everyone.

These statements seem contradictory, but they are not. They actually are in harmony. Both statements are from the Apostle Paul who wrote "For though I am free from all, I made myself a servant to all" (1 Corinthians 9:19) as well as "Owe no one anything, except to love each other" (Romans 13:8). To serve and obey whatever it loves is the very nature of love.

Christ was therefore free and enslaved. He was in the form of God[1] and the form of a servant.[2] Christ was Lord of all, but born of a woman, and born under the law.[3]

A Christian finds himself in much the same situation. A Christian has two natures: A spiritual nature and a bodily nature. When referring to the spiritual nature (which is also called the soul) a Christian is called the spiritual, the inner, or the new man. When referring to the bodily nature (which is also called the flesh) a Christian is called the body, the outer, or the old man.

10

The Apostle Paul refers to this two-fold nature of the Christian when he says: "Though our outer nature is wasting away, our inner nature is being renewed day by day" (2 Corinthians 4:16).

The reason why seemingly contradictory statements are often made in the Bible about Christians is due to the Christian's two-fold nature. The simple fact is that within each Christian two natures constantly oppose each other. "The flesh wars against the spirit and the spirit wars against the flesh" (Galatians 5:17).

[1]Cf. Philippians 2:6.
[2]Cf. Philippians 2:7.
[3]Cf. Galatians 4:4.

1. What two statements does Luther use to summarize *I Corinthians 9:19-23* and *Romans 13:8-10*?

2. How does Jesus describe faith in *John 4:13-14*?

3. According to *John 8:31,32*, how is a Christian truly liberated?

4. Whom ought the Christian's life be lived like (*I Corinthians 9:19*)?

5. What is the very nature of love (*I Corinthians 13:4-7*)?

6. We know the difference between the non-Christian life (*Ephesians 2:12*) and the Christian life (*Ephesians 2:13, 19-22*). But what goes on *within* the Christian (*Galatians 5:13-26*)?

2

LIVING IN FAITH

We begin by considering the inner man. There we will discover how a person is justified, liberated, and truly a Christian. Put another way: We'll understand how a Christian is truly a spiritual, new, and inner man.

First of all we must admit that absolutely no situation in life has any power to produce Christian righteousness or freedom. It also has no power to produce unrighteousness or bondage.

This fact can be demonstrated with a simple argument: What benefit is it to the soul if the body in which it resides is healthy, enjoys political freedom, and lives a fulfilling life by eating and drinking whatever it likes, and doing whatever it wants? The most un-Christian person addicted to every kind of vice does the same thing.

On the other hand: How is the soul harmed by a body which is diseased, enslaved, and experiences hunger, thirst and every other type of external evil? Even the best Christian who enjoys a clear conscience is forced to deal with such things. It is obvious then that neither of these outward circumstances in life can have anything to do with either the freedom or the bondage of the soul.

If a human body would be clothed with an alb, live in a monastery, busy itself with good works, pray, fast, and avoid eating meats—in short, do whatever it can do as a body—such outward acts would not, ultimately, be of spiritual benefit to the soul. Since any non-Christian could do such bodily acts as well, the only result of a dedication to them would be hypocrisy.

The Gospel is the only thing needed for life, justification and Christian freedom

The soul will not be injured if the body is clothed in ordinary clothing, lives in an ordinary house, eats an ordinary diet, prays silently, and does none of the things mentioned above. Such things could easily be done by hypocrites. *Something drastically different than such outward actions is needed to justify and free the soul.*

What about theological speculation? Meditation? Other exertions of the soul? Even these are of no spiritual benefit to the soul.

Only one thing is needed for life, justification and Christian freedom: The most holy Word of God, the Gospel of Jesus Christ. Christ Himself says: "I am the resurrection and the life. Whoever believes in me, though he die, yet shall he live" (John 11:25); "So if the Son sets you free, you will be free indeed" (John 8:36); "Man shall not live by bread alone, but by every word that comes from the mouth of God" (Matthew 4:4).

The soul can do without anything except the Word of God. Without the Word of God the soul receives absolutely nothing that it needs. With the Word of God the soul is rich and needs nothing else.

The Word of God is life, truth, light, peace, justification, salvation, joy, freedom, wisdom, virtue, grace, glory and everything good. For this reason the prophet, in Psalm 119 as well as in many other places, yearns for and calls upon the Word of God with many groans and sighs.

No expression of the wrath of God is more devastating than a famine of His Word (Amos 8:11).[1] No expression of the favor of God is greater than the sending forth of His Word, as it is written, "He sent out His Word and healed them, and delivered them from their destruction" (Psalm 107:20).

Jesus Christ was sent for no other work than that of the Word. The office of apostle, bishop and the ministry in general was instituted and established for no other reason than the ministry of the Word of God.

Now you might ask at this point: "What is this Word? There are so many 'Words of God'! What is the use of this particular Word of God?"

The Word of God, the Apostle Paul explains in Romans 1, is the *Good News of God* about *His Son*, the *Christ*, who became man, suffered, rose, and was *glorified through the Holy Spirit*, the Sanctifier.[2] When Christ is preached the soul is fed, justified, set free, and saved (if the soul believes such preaching).

Salvation is through the effective use of the Word of God and faith alone. Paul states to the Romans: "If you confess with your mouth that Jesus is Lord and believe in your heart that God raised him from the dead, you will be saved" (Romans 10:9); "Christ is the end of the law for righteousness to everyone who believes" (Romans 10:4); "The righteous shall live by faith" (Romans 1:17).

The Word of God cannot be received and revered by any works, but solely by faith. The soul needs the Word of God alone for life and justification. The soul is justified by faith alone and not by works. If the soul could be justified in any other way, it would need neither the Word of God nor faith.

Faith cannot coexist with works. If you believe that you can be justified by the works that you do, faith is of no value to you. If you would do such a thing, it would be like "vacillating between two religions"[3]: Either worshipping Baal or relying completely upon yourself—a great iniquity according to Job.[4]

Consequently, having come to faith, you learn that everything within you is utterly guilty, sinful, and damnable, as it is written, "For all have sinned and fall short of the glory of God" (Romans 3:23); and also,

"None is righteous, no, not one; no one understands; no one seeks for God. All have turned aside; together they have become worthless; no one does good, not even one" (Romans 3:10-12). When you have understood this, you will know that Christ is necessary for you.

It is Christ who suffered and rose again for you so that by believing in Him, you might by faith become a different person. Being justified by the work of another—namely Christ—all your sins have been forgiven.

Since Christian faith alone can reign in the inner man (as Paul writes in Romans "For with the heart one believes and is justified" (10:10)) and since faith alone justifies, no outward work or labor can justify the inner man. Neither can any outward work free or save the inner man. Works have no relation whatsoever to the inner man.

Works have no relation whatsoever to the inner man

Likewise it is only by impiety and unbelief in the heart that the inner man becomes guilty and a servant of sin deserving condemnation. No outer sin or work causes this.

The first concern of every Christian therefore should be to put aside all reliance upon such works. The Christian should strengthen his faith more and more and by it grow not in knowledge of works, but in knowledge of Jesus Christ who suffered and rose again for him. This is what Peter himself teaches (1 Peter 5:10) when he makes no other work than faith a Christian work.[5]

When the Jews asked Jesus what was necessary to do

the works of God, He rejected the works which He knew were the source of their arrogance, and demanded just one thing, saying: "This is the work of God, that you believe in him whom he has sent..." (John 6:29) "...for on Him God the Father has set his seal" (John 6:27).

Obviously, then, a genuine faith in Christ is a matchless treasure which results in universal salvation and preservation from evil, as it is written, "Whoever believes and is baptized will be saved, but whoever does not believe will be condemned" (Mark 16:16). Considering the treasure of the Gospel, Isaiah prophesied "Destruction is decreed, overflowing with righteousness. For the Lord God of hosts will make a full end, as decreed, in the midst of all the earth" (Isaiah 10:22-23). This is just as if Isaiah had said, "Faith, which is the brief and complete fulfilling of the law, will fill those who believe with such righteousness that they will need nothing else for justification." The Apostle Paul says the same thing: "For with the heart one believes and is justified" (Romans 10:10).

Genuine faith in Christ is a matchless treasure which results in universal salvation

But how can faith alone justify and give us such a fortune of marvelous things without works, when the Scriptures themselves demand a multitude of works, rituals and laws? The answer? First and foremost read what I have already asserted: Faith alone justifies, liberates and saves without works.

[1] "'Behold, the days are coming,' declares the Lord God, 'when I will send a famine on the land–not a famine of bread, nor a thirst for water, but of hearing the words of the Lord.'"

[2] Cf. Romans 1:1-4.

[3] 1 Kings 18:21.

[4] "If I have looked at the sun when it shone, or the moon moving in splendor, and my heart has been secretly enticed and my mouth has kissed my hand, this also would be an iniquity to be punished by the judges, for I would have been false to God above" Job 31:26-28.

[5] "And after you have suffered a little while, the God of all grace, who has called you to his eternal glory in Christ, will himself restore, confirm, strengthen, and establish you."

---

1. What warning does Jesus give in *Luke 12:22*?

2. What is the Christian's body (*I Corinthians 6:19*)?

3. What ought the Christian be doing (*I Timothy 4:7,8*)?

4. What role does food play in the life of the Christian (*I Corinthians 8:8* and *Romans 14:17*)?

5. What if a non-Christian prepares himself bodily (*Matthew 9:13* and *Hosea 6:6*)?

6. What two parts comprise the Christian (*II Corinthians 5:8*)?

7. What does the Word of God do to the Christian (*Romans 10:9,10, I Peter 2:2*, and *Job 23:12*)?

8. How does the psalmist speak of the Word in *Psalm 119:103,105,111,130*?

9. What will the salvation of the Word do (*II Chronicles 36:16*)?

10. Compare *II Chronicles 36:16* to *Romans 15:4*.

11. What does God think of our neglect of His Word (*II Chronicles 36:16*)?

12. What is the connection between Christ and His Word (*John 1:16*)?

13. What is the connection between the prophets and apostles and the Word of Christ (*Deuteronomy 4:10* and *II Corinthians 5:18*)?

14. What is the necessity of Christ (*Galatians 3:22–25* and *Romans 8:1-4,12-14*)?

15. So how important is a simple Christian faith (*Romans 3:28*)?

3

LAW AND PROMISE

The Word of God in general contains just two teachings. These teachings are the Law and the Promise. The law teaches us what is good. It does not, however, accomplish what it teaches.

The law shows us what we should do but does not give us the power to do it. The law was established to show man himself. Through the law a person is shown his own powerlessness to do any good. The law forces a person to abandon the idea that he, in fact, has the strength to fulfill the law.

Because the law works in such a fashion, it is called

the Old Testament. For example, "You shall not covet"[1] is a law by which we are all convicted of sin. No person can stop coveting—even if he tries extremely hard to do so. In order that a person may fulfill the law, and not covet, he is forced to abandon the thought that he is able to avoid coveting. He must look elsewhere for help to do so. This is what the prophet Hosea was getting at when he wrote: "He destroys you, O Israel, for you are against me, against your helper" (13:9).

What is done by just this one law is done by them all. All of the laws of God are equally impossible for us to fulfill.

When a person has been taught his own powerlessness by the law, he becomes concerned about the way he will fulfill the law. After all, the law must be fulfilled. *No jot or tittle of it can pass away.*[2] If a jot or tittle does pass away, a person has not fulfilled the law and is condemned. Realizing that he has no ability to fulfill the law, a person finds in himself no reason for his justification or salvation.

At this point, the other part of the Word of God, God's promises, enters. The promises of God declare the glory of God saying: "If you want to fulfill the law and not covet, believe in Christ! In Christ, God's undeserved love is promised to you as well as justification, peace, and liberty!"

All of these things will be yours if you believe. None of these things will be yours if you do not believe.

What is impossible for you to do by all the works of law—which are many and useless—is easily and completely possible through faith. God the Father has made everything depend upon faith.

Whoever has faith has everything. Whoever does not have faith has nothing. "For God has consigned all to disobedience, that he may have mercy on all" (Romans 11:32).

The promises of God give what the law demands and fulfill what the law commands. God alone does everything: The law and the fulfilling of the law. God alone commands. God alone fulfills.

> **God alone does everything. God alone commands. God alone fulfills.**

The promises of God therefore belong to the New Testament. Better yet: The promises of God *are* the New Testament.

Because the promises of God are words of holiness, truth, righteousness, liberty, and peace, and are full of universal goodness, the soul clings to them with a firm faith. The soul is united to them. The soul is thoroughly absorbed by the promises of God, so that it not only takes part in all of their virtues, but is penetrated and saturated by them.

If the touch of Christ healed, how much more would His tender spiritual touch—the Word truly absorbed—give to the soul all that His Word possesses? It is in this way, therefore, that the soul, alone through faith, without works, is justified from the Word of God. It is justified, sanctified, clothed with truth, peace, and liberty, filled completely with every good thing, and truly made a child of God. So John writes: "But to all who did receive him, who believed in his name, he gave the right to become children of God" (John 1:12).

[1]Cf. Exodus 20:17.

[2]Cf. Matthew 5:18: "For truly, I say to you, until heaven and earth pass away, not an iota, not a dot, will pass from the Law until all is accomplished."

———

1. What does the Law do for us (*Romans 7:12-14*)?

2. Does the Law give us strength to *fulfill* the Law itself (*Isaiah 4:6* and *I John 1:8*)?

3. What is the result of breaking just one Law (*James 2:10*)?

4. Is there any Law that is easier to fulfill (*Romans 7:7*)?

5. How perfectly are we to fulfill the Law (*Matthew 5:18*)?

6. So can we justify ourselves (*Galatians 3:24*)?

7. Can God justify us (*Philippians 3:9, Romans 5:1-5,* and *Romans 7:24,25*)?

8. What promises do we have in *John 20:31*?

9. In view of such a promise what does our soul possess (*I John 5:13* and *Romans 15:4*)?

4

CHARACTERISTICS OF FAITH

The *first characteristic of faith* is that it alone justifies the Christian. No good works, not even all the good works ever done piled on top of each other, can compare with faith.

No work can cleave to the Word of God or be found in the soul. Only faith and the Word of God are found in the soul.

As iron exposed to fire glows like the fire because of its union with it, so is the soul fashioned by the Word of God. Therefore faith accomplishes everything for the Christian.

The Christian needs no works of the law for his justification. Needing no works, he does not need the law. If the Christian does not need the law, he obviously is free from the law. So the Apostle Paul can write, "The law is not laid down for the just" (1 Timothy 1:9).

Faith then is, in reality, the freedom of the Christian. Through faith we do not become careless or lead an evil life, but cease to need the law or works for our justification and salvation.

A *second characteristic of faith* is that it honors Him in whom it believes. Christian faith honors Christ with the highest reverence and greatest repute.

Faith does this by believing that Christ is truthful and worthy of being believed. There is no greater honor than the reputation of truth and righteousness which we grant Him in whom we believe. In what higher esteem can we hold anyone than to think of Him as possessing truth, righteousness and absolute goodness? On the other hand, it is the greatest insult to consider someone to be false and unrighteous, or even to suspect him of such things, as we do when we do not believe him.

Faith is the freedom of the Christian

The soul, by believing the promises of God, considers Him to be true and righteous. The soul can give to God no higher glory than to think of Him as being true and righteous.

In fact, the highest worship of God is to ascribe to Him truth, righteousness, and any other qualities we would ascribe to one in whom we believe. When the soul thinks of God in this way, it demonstrates that it is prepared to do His will. In doing God's will the soul hallows God's name. In doing God's will the soul demonstrates that it is willing to be dealt with as it may please God.

You see, the soul simply clings to the promises of God and never doubts that God is true, just, wise, and

> **In doing God's will the soul hallows God's name**

will do, arrange and provide for everything that is needed in the best way possible. Is not a soul that believes in such a way most obedient to God in all things? Which commandment is not fulfilled by such obedience? What greater fulfillment of the law is there than complete obedience? Such obedience is not accomplished by works, but only by faith.

We can also think of this subject in this way: What greater defiance, impiety, or insult can there be to God than not to believe His promises? Are we not thinking of God as a liar and doubting His truth? Are we not attributing truth to ourselves and deception and frivolity to God? Are we not simply denying God and setting ourselves up as an idol in our hearts? If this truly is our spiritual state, if we truly are so impious, what can any works at all profit us—even if they are comparable to the works of angels and apostles?

Understandably God has consigned us all, not to wrath or lust, but to unbelief.[1] He has done this so that those who pretend they are fulfilling the law by pure and benevolent works (certainly social and human virtues!)

cannot presume that they will be saved. Instead, having also been included in the sin of unbelief, such people may either seek the mercy of God or be justly condemned.

When God, however, sees that we consider Him to be true, and that through the faith in our hearts He is honored with all the honor of which He is worthy, God, in response, honors us! On account of faith in Him, God honors us by considering us also to be true and righteous.

Faith itself is true and righteous when it ascribes to God what is His

Faith itself is true and righteous when it ascribes to God what is His. In return, God glorifies our righteousness. It simply is true and righteous that God is true and righteous. To confess this fact and ascribe to God these attributes is to be true and righteous ourselves. So He says, "For those who honor Me, I will honor, and those who despise Me shall be lightly esteemed" (1 Samuel 2:30). Paul says that Abraham's faith was *counted to him as righteousness*.[2] Why? Because by it he gave glory to God. For the very same reason the same thing will happen to us—we shall be counted righteous if we believe.

A *third characteristic of faith* is that it unites the soul of the Christian to Christ. In a similar fashion to the union of husband and wife (which is 'mysterious' in the words of the Apostle Paul[3]) so too does the soul of the Christian and Christ become one flesh.

If the soul of the Christian and Christ are one flesh, and a true marriage exists between them (realize that we are thinking of the most perfect of all marriages—human marriages are but poor examples of this one great marriage!), whatever each possesses becomes the common property of both. Both good things as well as bad things! This means that whatever belongs to Christ becomes the possession of the Christian soul and it can boast about it as if it were his own! Whatever is the possession of the Christian soul Christ takes to be His own.

In comparison then, it is obvious that the Christian soul, through this marriage, has experienced an incalculable gain of possessions. Christ is full of grace, life, and salvation. The soul is full of sin, death and condemnation.

Through faith, sin, death and hell become possessions of Christ. Through faith grace, life and salvation become possessions of the soul. Being the Husband, Christ must take responsibility for what belongs to the wife. At the same time, He gives to the wife what is His. If He gives His wife His own body and Himself, how can Christ *not* give her all that

> **Whatever is the possession of the Christian soul Christ takes to be His own**

He possesses? If He takes to Himself the body of His wife, how can Christ not also take to Himself all that is hers as well?

In this marriage of the soul of the Christian to Christ a delightful vision is given to us. It is a vision not only of communion, but of successful warfare, victory, salvation and redemption. Christ is God and man. Christ is the

Person who has not sinned, will not die, and will not be condemned. Indeed Christ cannot sin, die or be condemned. The righteousness, life and salvation Christ possesses are invincible, eternal and almighty.

When I say that Christ is a Person who through the wedding ring of faith becomes a part of the sin, death and hell of His wife—no, even better, He makes them His possession—what I mean is that Christ deals with them in no other way than if they actually were His and He Himself had sinned. When Christ suffered, died, and descended into hell, He did so to overcome all things. Sin, death, and hell could not swallow Christ up. In a stupendous conflict, Christ swallowed up sin, death and hell. After all, Christ's righteousness rises above the sins of every man. Christ's life is more powerful than death. Christ's salvation is unconquerable by hell.

Obviously then, the believing soul, through faith in Christ, becomes free of all sin, unafraid of death, and safe from hell. The soul is also given the eternal righteousness, life, and salvation which belongs to its Husband Christ. In this way Christ presents to Himself a glorious bride, without spot or wrinkle, *cleansing her with the washing of water with the Word,*[4] that is, by faith in the word of life, righteousness, and salvation. In such a way Christ initiates the engagement of the Christian soul to Himself "in faithfulness, in righteousness and in justice,

> **The soul is also given the eternal righteousness, life, and salvation which belongs to its Husband Christ**

in steadfast love and mercy" (Hosea 2:19,20).

Who can estimate the true value of this royal wedding? Who can even comprehend the worth of the glory of this grace? Christ, the rich and pious Husband, marries a poor and impious prostitute. In doing so, Christ rescues her from all her evil and gives to her all His good things. This having been done, it is now impossible that she will be destroyed for her sins. Her sins have become the possession of Christ and assumed by Him. Having in her husband, Christ, a righteousness which now she can claim as her own and can erect opposite all her sins, death and hell, she can claim: "Even if I have sinned, my husband, Christ, in whom I believe, has not sinned. Everything that belongs to me has become His possession. All His possessions have become mine." So we read: "My beloved is mine, and I am His" (Song of Solomon 2:16); and Paul writes: "But thanks be to God, Who gives us the victory through our Lord Jesus Christ" (1 Corinthians 15:57). This 'victory' about which Paul writes is a victory over sin and death (1 Corinthians 15:57).

It should be obvious why so much importance is attributed to faith. Faith alone can fulfill the law and justify with works. The First Commandment[5], "You shall have no other Gods," is fulfilled alone by faith. If you were nothing but good works from the bottom of your feet to the top of your head you would not be worshiping God, nor fulfilling the First Commandment. It is impossible to worship God without attributing to Him the glory of truth and universal goodness. This is not done by work but by faith in the heart. It is not by working, but by believing, that we glorify God and confess Him to be true. Faith alone is the righteousness of the Christian and the fulfilling of all the commandments.

Faith alone is the righteousness of the Christian and the fulfilling of all the commandments

Whoever fulfills the First Commandment easily completes the rest.

Works, being dead things, cannot glorify God. If faith is present, however, works can be done to the glory of God.

The topic before us is not the quality of works, but what actually does them and glorifies God with them. Faith of the heart does such works. Faith is the sum and substance of all our righteousness.

It is an ineffective and dangerous doctrine which teaches that the commandments are fulfilled by works. The commandments had to have been fulfilled *before* any good works could be done. Good works are done *after* the fulfillment of the law.

[1]"For God has consigned all to disobedience, that he may have mercy on all" Romans 11:32.

[2]"For if Abraham was justified by works, he has something to boast about, but not before God. For what does the Scripture say? [Genesis 15:6] 'Abraham believed God, and it was counted to him as righteousness.'" Romans 4:2-3.

[3]Cf. Ephesians 5:32.

[4]Cf. Ephesians 5:26-27.

[5]Cf. Exodus 20:3

1. Can our own actions help in justifying us (*Philippians 3:8,9*)? How about faith (*Philippians 4:13*)?

2. According to *John 8:31,32* and *Philippians 1:20,21*, what do Christians have?

3. What credit are we to give to God (*I Chronicles 16:23-29,36*)?

4. What ought we be ready to do then (*I Chronicles 29:3,11* and *Romans 12:2*)?

5. How do we feel about God (*Isaiah 2:3, Psalms 23:6,* and *Psalms 95:6*)?

6. How does God see us now (*II Corinthians 5:18,19*)?

7. How does our righteousness look now (*Romans 4:2,3* and *Romans 3:21-24*)?

8. To what extent are we united to Christ (*Ephesians 2:28-32*)?

9. What does Christ share with us (*Colossians 3;1-4,12-14* and *I Peter 2:24*)?

10. How are we clothed spiritually through Christ (*Romans 13:14, Philippians 1:11,* and *Ephesians 6:14*)?

11. What did Christ assume for us (*Isaiah 53:4,6*) and what does He give us (*Romans 4:23–5:5*)?

12. Then why do we want to act in a God-pleasing way (*I Timothy 6:11* and *John 15:5-8,16*)?

5

CHRIST THE FIRSTBORN: PRIEST AND KING

A panoramic view of the grace given our inner man in Christ is found in the Old Testament. There we read that God sanctified to Himself every first-born male.[1]

This birthright was of the greatest value. It gave the first-born male the right of superiority over the rest of the children by the double honor of priesthood and kingship.[2] The first-born male was both priest and lord of all the others.

The first-born male foreshadowed Christ. Christ was the true first-born of God the Father and the virgin Mary.[3] Christ was a true king and priest, but not in a fleshly and earthly sense. His kingdom *is not of this world*.[4] Christ reigns and acts as priest in heavenly and spiritual things such as righteousness, truth, wisdom, peace, and salvation.[5] All things on earth and in hell are subject to Christ.[6] How could he defend us from them if they were not? But it is not *in* the things of earth and hell, nor *by* these things, that Christ's kingdom stands.

> **Christ was a true King and Priest, but not in a fleshly and earthly sense**

The priesthood of Christ does not consist of outward displays of vestments and rituals. Such things belong to the human priesthood of Aaron[7] and the ecclesiastical priesthood of today.

The priesthood of Christ consists of spiritual things. In these spiritual things, in an office invisible to us, Christ intercedes before God in heaven for us.[8] It is there that Christ offers Himself and performs all the duties of an earthly priest. (Paul describes such a priesthood to the Hebrews using the figure of Melchizedek.[9])

Christ not only prays and intercedes for us in heaven, but He also teaches us inwardly in our spirits with the living teachings of His Spirit.[10] These are the two special responsibilities of a priest, as demonstrated by human priests in their visible prayers and sermons.

---

[1]Cf. Exodus 13:1-2, 12-13, 15; 22:29-30. Cf. Luke 2:23.
[2]Cf. Genesis 25:29-34; Cf. Hebrews 12:16.
[3]Cf. Luke 1:26-35.
[4]Cf. John 18:33-38.

[5]Cf. Hebrews 7ff.

[6]Cf. Matthew 28:18; Hebrews 1; 1 Peter 3:22.

[7]Cf. Exodus 28-29.

[8]"The former priests were many in number, because they were prevented by death from continuing in office, but he holds his priesthood permanently, because he continues forever. Consequently, he is able to save to the uttermost those who draw near to God through him, since he always lives to make intercession for them" Hebrews 7:23-25. Cf. Hebrews 4:14-5:10 and John 17.

[9]Cf. Hebrews 7.

[10]"But the Helper, the Holy Spirit, whom the Father will send in my name, he will teach you all things and bring to your remembrance all that I have said to you." John 14:26.

---

1. Who really was Christ (*Luke 1:35*)?

2. How was He Priest (*Hebrews 9:11-14*)?

3. Some believe Christ is going to set up His Kingdom here on earth. What did He say about that (*John 18:36*)?

4. What do *I Peter 3:22, Colossians 1:18,* and *Ephesians 1:22* say about Christ's authority?

5. What is Jesus doing for all of us according to *I John 2:2*?

6. For what purpose did He send us the Spirit (*John 14:26*)?

6

THE CHRISTIAN:
PRIEST AND KING

By His birth Christ has assumed the offices of priest and king. He grants both to every believer in Him through the spiritual matrimony described above. In that marriage, all that is the husband's becomes the wife's.

All who believe in Christ, therefore, are kings and priests in Christ. As it is written: "But you are a chosen race, a royal priesthood, a holy nation, a people for his own possession, that you may proclaim the excellencies of him who called you out of darkness into his marvelous light" (1 Peter 2:9).

The Christian's work as both king and priest is to be

understood in the following way. First, insofar as every Christian is a king, every Christian is by faith exalted above all things. In spiritual power, therefore, the Christian is completely lord of all things earthly. Nothing whatever can do him any harm. All things are subject to him and are compelled to serve him for his salvation.

> **All things are subject to the Christian and are compelled to serve him for his salvation**

Paul therefore says: "for those who love God all things work together for good, for those who are called according to his purpose" (Romans 8:28), and also, "Whether...the world or life or death or the present or the future—all are yours, and you are Christ's" (1 Corinthians 3:22,23).

In no way whatsoever has one specific Christian been chosen to possess and to rule all things in the worldly sense of the term. This is simply the misguided and senseless idea of certain churchmen.

Such a worldly reign is the work of kings, princes and men upon the earth. In the world common sense tells us that we are subjected to all things, suffer many things, and even die. The fact of the matter is that the more Christian any person is, the more he will be subject to evils, sufferings and death. So was the case with Christ the First-born and all the holy brethren.

The reign of the Christian is a spiritual reign, which rules in the presence of enemies and is powerful at the moment of distress. The reign of the Christian is nothing else than that *strength which is made perfect in...weakness.*[1]

It is a reign which arranges all things for the benefit of my salvation. Even the cross and death are compelled to serve me and to work for my salvation. The reign of the Christian is lofty and eminent in dignity, and a true and almighty dominion. It is a spiritual empire in which there is nothing so good, and nothing so bad, that it will not *work together for my good*—if only I believe.[2]

Faith alone suffices for my salvation. I need nothing except to exercise the power and reign of the liberty of faith. This is the incalculable power and freedom of Christians.

Not only are Christians kings and the freest people of all, but also priests forever. This is a dignity far greater than kingship. By this priesthood a Christian is worthy to appear before God, to pray for others, and to teach others about God. These are the duties of priests and in no way should be permitted to be fulfilled by an unbeliever.

Believing in Christ, Christ has obtained for us this status: As we are His brothers and coheirs and fellow-kings, so also are we His fellow-priests. Through the spirit of faith we can venture with confidence into the presence of God, and cry, "Abba, Father!".[3] We can also pray for each other and do all the other things we have seen done and

> **I need nothing except to exercise the power and reign of the liberty of faith**

foreshadowed in the visible and worldly office of the priesthood.

If someone were not to believe in Christ, nothing would render his service or work for good. The unbeliever is a slave to all things and all things turn out for his evil. This is because he uses all things in an impious way for his own advantage and not for the glory of God.

An unbeliever is in no way a priest but an unholy person whose prayers are sin. The unbeliever never appears in the presence of God simply because God does not hear sinners.[4]

What then can compare to the greatness of that Christian nobility which by its royal power rules over all things—even death, life and sin? What can compare to the priestly glory of the Christian? Before God it is all-powerful. God Himself will do what the Christian seeks and wishes, as it is written: "He fulfills the desire of those who fear him; he also hears their cry and saves them." (Psalm 145:19).

Such glory is not achieved by works, but only by faith. Obviously, then, anyone can clearly see how a Christian is free from everything. He does not need good works to be justified and saved. The Christian receives these gifts in abundance from faith alone.

If a Christian were so naive as even to pretend that he is justified, released, saved and made a Christian by any good work, he would instantly lose faith and all its benefits. It would be like in the fable where a dog, carrying a piece of meat in his mouth, is fooled by its reflection in water. In its attempt to get the meat that it sees in the reflection, the dog loses both the real meat and that of the reflection.

[1]Cf. 2 Corinthians 12:8-9.

[2]Cf. Romans 8:28.

[3]Cf. Mark 14:36; Romans 8:15; Galatians 4:6.

[4]"We know that God does not listen to sinners, but if anyone is a worshipper of God and does his will, God listens to him." John 9:31.

---

1. Describe in your own words what Peter writes in *I Peter 2:5-10.*

2. What are we according to *II Timothy 2:12?*

3. What can we expect (*James 1:2-4*)?

4. How are we to carry on (*II Corinthians 12:7-10*)?

5. What is the power and yet freedom of a Christian (*II Corinthians 3:17, John 8:32, Micah 3:8,* and *Acts 4:33*)?

6. What do Christians have as priests (*I Peter 2:9*), those who pray (*Ephesians 6:18*), and teachers (*II Timothy 3:16,17*)?

7. Do unbelievers have these things (*Romans 8:5-8*)?

8. How do we receive these gifts (*John 15:7*)?

7

PASTORS AND PREACHING

At this point you are probably thinking: "If all Christians are priests, what is the difference between my pastor and me?" My answer is simply that the common usage of words such as 'priest,' 'clergy,' 'spiritual person,' and 'ecclesiastic' is not helpful, since it gives titles to a few within the church which really should be applied to all Christians.

The Word of God makes no such distinction except that those who are now called popes, bishops and leaders, it calls ministers, servants and stewards. Such ministers, servants and stewards are to serve the rest of the body of

Christ with the ministry of the Word, the teaching of the faith of Christ, and the liberty of believers.

Although it is true that we are all priests, we cannot and, even if we could, should not, all minister and teach publicly. So Paul says, "This is how one should regard us, as servants of Christ and stewards of the mysteries of God" (1 Corinthians 4:1).

The ecclesiastical structure we have now is the result of an arrogant display of power and such a terrible despotism that no earthly government is like it. It is as if the laity were anything but Christians. Through such exploitation of the Church the knowledge of grace, faith, liberty and Christ has completely disappeared. It has been replaced by insufferable enslavement to manmade works and laws. According to Lamentations (5:7-9) we have become the slaves of the worst men on earth. Such men take advantage of our misery for the disgraceful and shameful purposes of their own will.

Returning to the subject with which we began, I think it has become clear by what I have said that it is not enough, nor even Christian, to preach about the works, life and words of Christ merely as a matter of history (the knowledge of which is sufficient to direct our lives). The most popular preachers today preach about Christ in this way. Others ignore the historical life of Christ altogether and preach about man-made laws and the sayings of the Fathers. Still other preachers preach about Christ with the goal of stirring human emotions to sympathize with Christ, to become angry with the Jews, and all sorts of other childish absurdities.

The object of preaching should be the promotion of faith in Christ: Faith that Jesus is not only the Christ, but the Christ *for you and for me*. Whatever is preached about Christ should be preached so that what is said about Him, and what He is called, works within us.

Such faith is a result of and maintained by preaching why God became man in Christ, what Christ has brought us and given to us, and to what profit and advantage is His reception. Proper preaching *proclaims* the Christian liberty we

> **Proper preaching proclaims the Christian liberty we have in Christ**

have in Christ, *demonstrates* the way in which we Christians are kings, priests and lords of all things, and *explains* how we can be confident that whatever we do in the presence of God is pleasing and acceptable to Him.

Who would not rejoice in his most inmost being at hearing such things? Who, having heard news of such great comfort, would not himself be filled with the love of Christ—a love which can never be attained by any laws or works? What could injure or frighten such a person? If the consciousness of sin or the horror of death were to come upon him, he is prepared, hoping in the Lord, unfearing and undisturbed, waiting until he shall look down upon his enemies.

Such a Christian believes that the righteousness of Christ is his own. He also believes that his sin is no longer his own but is now Christ's. On account of faith in Christ a Christian's sin has been swallowed up by the righteousness of Christ, as I have said above. Such a

Christian learns with the Apostle to scoff at sin and death, and to say, "O death, where is your victory? O death, where is your sting? The sting of death is sin, and the power of sin is the law. But thanks be to God, who gives us the victory through our Lord Jesus Christ" (1 Corinthians 15:55-57).

Death certainly is swallowed up in victory, but not only in the victory of Christ. Death is also swallowed up in our victory, since by faith Christ's victory becomes ours and in it we too conquer.

This is enough now about the inner man and its liberty. Enough has also been said about the righteousness of faith which does not need either laws or good works. Indeed laws and good works can even be detrimental to faith, if a Christian were to think he is justified by them.

———

1. What are the tasks of Pastors according to *I Timothy 4:1-16, II Timothy 4:2-5,* and *Titus 1:7-9*?

2. What do false preachers do (*James 2:19*)?

3. What has to be central in Christian preaching (*Romans 5:8* and *I Timothy 1:15-17*)?

4. What has Christ brought us (*Romans 5:15-19*)?

5. What confidence should Christians have (*Hebrews 4:16* and *Hebrews 10:19-22*)?

6. What do Christians have now (*I Corinthians 1:30* and *Romans 8:35-37*)?

8

An Internal Struggle

So what about the outer man? Here we need to respond to those whom by this point may be thinking: "If faith does everything and by itself is enough for our justification, why does God command good works? Are we simply to relax and do nothing? Should we be content with faith alone?" My answers to these questions? No, no and no.

Now if we were thoroughly and completely inner and spiritual Christians that would certainly be the case. But such a spiritual state will not be seen again until the last day when the dead will rise again. As long as we still live we are simply making a beginning and advancing toward that which will be completed in our future life.

What we have now spiritually the Apostle calls the first fruits of the Spirit (Romans 8:23).[1] In the future we shall have everything and the fullness of the Spirit. This is the reason for stating what I have before: The Christian is the servant of all and subject to all. In that part in which he is free the Christian does no works. In that part in which he is a servant the Christian does nothing but works.

Let us examine why this is so. Inwardly, according to the spirit, a man is justified by faith, having everything he requires spiritually. This very faith and abundance ought to increase every day until the future life. Nevertheless the Christian remains in this mortal life on earth. In this mortal life it is necessary that he rule his own body and have interaction with other people.

This is where works begin. On this earth the Christian must not relax. Here he must exercise his body by fasting, keeping vigils, laboring, and other such regular disciplines.

The Christian does this so that the body is subdued by the spirit, obeys it, and is conformed to the inner man and faith. If it is not subdued in such a way, it is the nature of the body to rebel against both the inner man and faith and hinder them in any way it can.

The inner man, being conformed to God and recreated in His image through faith, rejoices and delights in Christ as the source of all the blessings and so really has only one thing it must do: Freely and joyously serve God in love.

When the inner man does this, however, it comes into conflict with the contrary will residing in his own flesh. The will of the flesh strives only to serve the world and seek its own gratification. The spirit of faith cannot and will not bear the will of the flesh, and so constantly strives with cheerfulness and zeal to keep it in submission and restrain it. This is why Paul writes:

> **The will of the flesh strives only to serve the world and seeks its own gratification**

"I delight in the law of God in my inner being; but I see in my members another law waging war against the law of my mind and making me captive to the law of sin" (Romans 7: 22, 23); "I discipline my body, and keep it under control, lest after preaching to others, I myself should be disqualified" (1 Corinthians 9:27); "Those who belong to Christ Jesus have crucified the flesh with its passions and desires" (Galatians 5:24).

Such works, however, must not be done with the thought that they can justify a man before God. Faith, which alone makes the Christian righteous before God, cannot bear this misconception.

---

[1]"And not only the creation, but we ourselves, who have the first fruits of the Spirit, groan inwardly as we wait eagerly for adoption as sons, the redemption of our bodies."

1. Is the Christian to be content with faith and not concern himself with works (*Ephesians 2:8-10*)?

2. Are we to keep striving to do better (*I Corinthians 9:25* and *Philippians 3:13,14*)?

3. Compare and summarize *Titus 3:5* and *I Timothy 6:8.*

4. How are we justified (*Romans 5:1*)?

5. What growth should we have (*II Peter 3:18*)?

6. What part does Christ play (*Romans 7:25*)?

7. And what is our response (*I John 3:16*)?

9

WORKING THE BODY
INTO SUBMISSION

The works of the Christian are for one purpose alone: To focus his efforts solely on bringing his body into submission and thus purify it from its sinful desires. The soul, cleansed by faith and loving God, would have all things cleansed in this same way—especially its own body—so that all may unite with it in loving and praising God.

Because of the basic requirements of his body, therefore, the Christian cannot relax, but must do many good works in order to keep it in submission. These works do not justify the Christian before God. The

Christian does them out of love, in service to God. The Christian does good works for no other purpose than to do what is well-pleasing to Him whom he desires to obey in all things.

Accordingly, it is up to each Christian to decide in what way and in what matter he should subjugate his own body. The Christian will fast, watch, and work to the extent needed to subdue the indecency and sensuality of the body.

> **It is up to each Christian to decide in what way and in what matter he should subjugate his own body**

Anyone pretending to be justified by such works, however, is not attempting to mortify his lusts, but to gain spiritual credit for what he is doing. "If only," such a person thinks, "such works can be accomplished, all will be well and I will be justified!"

Sometimes, however, such works can even do the body great physical harm, destroying it and making it useless. When anyone strives in such a way to justify and save himself, it is simply tragic, and is merely the result of a lack of knowledge of Christian faith and life.

---

1. What is the purpose of the works of Christians (*Romans 6:13* and *James 4:7*)?

2. What does *Hebrews 12:1* say to Christians?

3. What motivates Christians (*Psalms 40:8* and *Psalms 143:10*)?

10

WORKING IN THE GARDEN

Here is another way to look at the works of the outer man. The works of a Christian—already justified and saved by faith out of the pure and unmerited mercy of God—should be considered to be the same as those of Adam and Eve in paradise before the Fall. About these works we read that, "The Lord God took the man and put him into the Garden of Eden to work it and to keep it" (Genesis 2:15).

Now God created Adam just and righteous. Adam was not justified and made righteous by keeping the garden and working in it. God gave Adam the business of keeping and cultivating paradise simply for employment. Adam's works were works of perfect freedom, being done for no object but that of pleasing God. Adam's works were not done in order to obtain justification, which he already had completely.

The same is true for the works of a believer. Being placed again in paradise and recreated through faith, he needs no works for his justification. In order that he may not be idle, he exercises his own body and preserves it. The Christian's works are done freely, with the sole purpose of pleasing God.

> **Adam's works were not done in order to obtain justification, which he already had completely**

We, however, are not yet fully recreated in perfect faith and love. Faith and love, however, must increase. This is not done through works, but through themselves.

A bishop, when he consecrates a church building, confirms children, or carries out any other duty of his office, is not made a bishop by these works. Unless he had been previously consecrated as a bishop, not one of those works would have any validity. They would be foolish, childish, and silly. In the same way a Christian, being consecrated by his faith, does good works.

A Christian, however, is not made more of a Christian or a more sacred person by these works. Faith alone does this. Unless he is a believer and a Christian, none of his works have any value at all. His works would instead be impious and damnable sins.

These two sayings are therefore true: "Good works

do not make a good man, but a good man does good works;" "Bad works do not make a bad man, but a bad man does bad works."

A person must be good before any good works can be done. Good works follow and flow out of a good person. As Christ says, "A healthy tree cannot bear bad fruit, nor can a diseased tree bear good fruit" (Matthew 7:18). The fruit clearly does not bear the tree, nor does the tree grow on the fruit. The opposite is true: The tree bears fruit, and the fruit grows on the tree.

Since a tree must exist before its fruit, and since its fruit does not make the tree either good or bad, and since a good or bad tree produces fruit of the same kind respectively, so must first a person be good or bad before he can do either a good or a bad work. A person's works do not make him good or bad, but he himself makes his works either good or bad.

The same is true for carpenters. A bad or good house does not make a good or bad carpenter, but a good or bad carpenter builds a good or bad house.

In general, no work makes a worker reflect its quality. Instead, a worker makes the work such as he himself is.

The same is true for the works of people in general. As a person himself is—believing or unbelieving—such is his work. It is good if it is done in faith. It is bad if done in unbelief.

The opposite, however, is not true. It is not true that such as the work is, such the person becomes in faith or in unbelief. Works do not make a person believe. Neither do works justify a person. It is faith alone—in that it makes a person a believer and justified—which makes a person's works truly good.

Since works justify no one, but a person must be justified before he can do any good work, it is obvious that it is faith alone—created by the mercy of God through Christ by means of His Word—which worthily and sufficiently justifies and saves a person. A Christian man needs no work or law for his salvation.

By faith a Christian is free from all law. The Christian does what he does in perfect freedom and thanksgiving. A Christian does not seek profit or salvation from his works. By the grace of God the Christian through faith is already saved and has everything he needs. The Christian does works simply to please God.

No good work can justify an unbeliever or save him. No evil work makes an unbeliever evil and condemned. It is simply unbelief alone which makes a person and his works evil and ultimately condemns him. A man is not made good or bad by his works, but from his faith or unbelief. The saying then is true: "The beginning of sin is to fall away from God,"[1] that is, not to believe. Paul says, "Whoever would draw near to God must believe" (Hebrews 11:6). Christ says the same thing: "Either make the tree good and its fruit good, or make the tree bad and its fruit bad" (Matthew 12:33).

> **A man is not made good or bad by his works, but from his faith or unbelief**

What Christ means is simply that as whoever wants to have good fruit will begin with the tree, and plant a good tree, so too whoever wants to do good works must begin, not by working, but by believing. It is believing which makes a person good. Nothing makes a person good but faith. Nothing makes a person bad but unbelief.

To the world it appears otherwise. In the sight of most people, a person becomes good or evil by his works. The word 'becomes' here, however, must be rightly understood. It means that whoever ultimately is good or evil is eventually *seen* to be good or evil and *recognized* by everyone as good or evil.[2] Christ affirms this saying: "You will recognize them by their fruits" (Matthew 7:20).

All such recognition, however, stops at appearances and externals. In this matter many deceive themselves. They presume to write and teach that we are justified by good works. Meanwhile, they make no mention of faith. They walk in their own ways, always *deceived and ever deceiving*. They go from *bad to worse*,[3] the *blind leading the blind*,[4] wearing themselves out with works, and never attaining true righteousness. These are those of whom Paul says, "Having the appearance of godliness, but denying its power...always learning and never able to arrive at a knowledge of the truth" (2 Timothy 3:5,7).

Whoever does not wish to go astray following such blindness must look further than to the works of the law or the doctrine of works. Such a person should stop contemplating his works and consider himself and the way in which he may be justified.

A person is justified and saved, not by works or laws, but by the Word of God. What the 'Word of God' means here is the promise of the Grace of God. In so doing, all glory is given the Divine Majesty, Who has saved us not by works or righteousness,[5] but by His mercy, the Word of His grace.

[1]Cf. Sirach 10:14-15.

[2]"The sins of some men are conspicuous, going before them to judgment, but the sins of others appear later. So also good works are conspicuous, and even those that are not cannot remain hidden" 1 Timothy 5:24-25.

[3]Cf. 2 Timothy 3:13.

[4]Cf. Matthew 15:14; Luke 6:39.

[5]"He saved us, not because of works done by us in righteousness, but according to his own mercy, by the washing of regeneration and renewal of the Holy Spirit" Titus 3:5.

———————

1. What work is needed for justification (*Galatians 2:16*)?

2. Why do Christians work for the Lord (*Ephesians 6:7, Deuteronomy 10:12, II Timothy 1:3*, and *Psalms 40:8*)?

3. Have we reached perfection yet (*Philippians 3:12*)?

4. But what must increase (*Galatians 5:6, 13, 22-26*)?

5. So what part do good works play in the life of Christians (*I Corinthians 2:14, I Corinthians 12:3*, and *Matthew 7:15-20*)?

6. But what if those works are done in unbelief (*Matthew 25:35,36*)?

7. So once again: Why do Christians do good deeds (*I Peter 2:9*)?

11

WORKING UNDER A YOKE

By this point the reason for either shunning or embracing good works should be clear. A proper understanding of good works should also be apparent.

If works are understood to be the reason for our justification, if works are done with the misunderstanding that we can even pretend to be justified by them, then a yoke of necessity is laid upon us.[1] Such a yoke of necessity extinguishes both liberty and faith. When the proviso of *necessity* is added to works, they no longer can be considered good, and in reality, should be condemned.

The reason they should be condemned is that they are not freely done. They therefore blaspheme the very grace of God which alone is the reason we are saved and justified through faith. Works cannot do such a thing. Yet, being impiously presumptuous (and with our consent!), our works take it on themselves to achieve our justification. In so doing, they violently attack and seek to supplant the office and glory of the grace of God.

> **We do not reject good works... we, in fact, embrace them**

We do not reject good works. We, in fact, embrace them. We teach them constantly.

We do not condemn works on the basis of themselves, but on the basis of what impiously has been added to them: Their necessity in the quest for justification. Such additions cause works to be only good in outward show. But in reality works are not good, since by them men are deceived and deceive others just like *ravenous wolves* dressed up in *sheep's clothing*.[2]

When faith is absent, this monster,[3] this distorted notion about works, is invincible. There is no way doers of works can restrain it until faith, which destroys it, comes and reigns in the heart.

Nature does not have the power to expel such a monster. Indeed, nature cannot even see it for what it is, but instead, considers it to be a good and holy will. Throw in a dash of custom by means of an impious teacher or two, and this corruption of nature is greatly strengthened. The evil then becomes incurable. The multitudes are led astray to irreparable ruin.

Although it is good to preach and write about penitence, confession, and satisfaction, if we stop there and do not go on to teach faith, such teaching is without doubt deceitful and devilish. Christ, speaking by His servant John, not only said, "Repent," but added, "for the kingdom of heaven is at hand" (Matthew 3:2). Not one word of God alone, but both, should be preached. Both *old* and *new things* should be *brought out of the treasury*.[4] The voice of the law should be heard as well as the word of grace.

The voice of the law should be brought forward, that men might be terrified and brought to knowledge of their sins. They then would be moved to repentance and to a better manner of life. We must not, however, stop here. That would be equivalent to wounding and not binding up, striking and not healing, killing and not making alive, bringing down to hell and not bringing back up, humbling and not exalting. In order to teach and establish faith, the word of grace and of the promised forgiveness of sin must also be preached. Without contrition, penitence and all other duties are performed and taught in vain.

> **Without contrition, penitence and all other duties are performed and taught in vain**

Preachers of repentance and grace certainly are still to be found. Such preachers, however, do not explain the law and the promises of God with the goal and intent that people learn of the source of repentance and grace.

Repentance comes from the law of God. Faith or grace, however, comes from the promises of God, as it is said, "Faith comes from hearing, and hearing through the word of Christ" (Romans 10:17).

When a person is humbled and is confronted with the knowledge of himself by the threats and terrors of the law, he is consoled and raised up by faith in the divine promise. So "weeping may tarry for the night, but joy comes with the morning" (Psalm 30:5). This is enough now concerning works in general, and also concerning works which the Christian does in reference to his own body.

[1] Cf. Acts 15:10.

[2] Cf. Matthew 7:15.

[3] Reference here is to the Leviathan of Job 41.

[4] Cf. "And he said to them, 'Therefore every scribe who has been trained for the kingdom of heaven is like a master of a house, who brings out of his treasure what is new and what is old'" Matthew 13:52.

———————————

1. What was the reason for the Council in Jerusalem (*Acts 15:5-11*)?

2. Clarify Peter's words in *vv. 10,11*.

3. What do good deeds do if done without faith in Christ (*Romans 11:6, Titus 3:5,* and *Galatians 4:8-11*)?

4. Note Paul's desire in *Romans 10:1* and how others could get it (*Romans 10:17*). What is Paul talking about (*Romans 11:6*)?

5. Why can the cults become so popular (*Colossians 2:20-23*)?

6. Where do the Law and Gospel fit in (*Luke 3:7-10,18*)?

7. Note John's preaching (*Matthew 3:1,2,6,8-10*). What did Jesus say about it (*Matthew 11:7-10*)?

8. What did Paul say about preaching in *II Timothy 4:1-5?*

9. Note how Peter's sermon after Pentecost contains both Law (*Acts 2:22-24*) and Gospel (*Acts 2:36-39*).

10. Why is *Jude 24, 25* so comforting?

12

WORKING FOR YOUR NEIGHBOR

A Christian does not live in his body merely for himself and to improve himself. A Christian lives for all people on earth.

In fact, a Christian lives not for himself at all, but only for others. It is in order to serve others more sincerely and freely that a Christian brings his body into submission. This is why Paul says, "None of us lives to himself, and none of us dies to himself. If we live, we live to the Lord, and if we die, we die to the Lord" (Romans 14:7,8).

It is impossible for a Christian to live a life of ease

and not work for the good of his neighbor. The Christian must speak, act and interact with other people just as Jesus Christ Himself was *made in the likeness of men* and *found in fashion as a man*,[1] and conversed with men.

Still a Christian needs to do none of these things for his justification and salvation. Rather, the Christian should have one goal and purpose in all his works: To serve and be useful to others in all that he does.

The Christian should think of nothing else than the maintenance and improvement of his neighbor. This is why the Apostle Paul commands us to work with our own hands: That we may be able to give to those in need.[2] He might have said, that we may support ourselves. Instead, he tells us to give to those in need.[3]

> **A Christian should have one goal : to serve and be useful to others in all that he does**

The Christian takes care of his own body in order that, through its health, he is able to work and to acquire and preserve property in order to help those who are in need. In this way the stronger member serves the weaker member,[4] and we become the children of God,[5] thinking of and working for each other, *bearing one another's burdens*, and so *fulfilling the law of Christ.*[6]

This is truly the Christian life. This is *faith* really *working through love*[7]: When a Christian, being himself abundantly satisfied by the fullness and riches of his own faith, joyously and lovingly serves others voluntarily and freely without reward.

This is why the Apostle Paul, having taught the

Philippians how they had been made rich by that faith in Christ in which they had obtained all things, taught them further:

"So if there is any encouragement in Christ, any comfort from love, any participation in the Spirit, any affection and sympathy, complete my joy, by being of the same mind, having the same love, being in full accord and of one mind. Do nothing from rivalry or conceit, but in humility count others more significant than yourselves. Let each of you look not only to his own interests, but also to the interest of others." (Philippians 2:1-4).

Here the Apostle clearly establishes this maxim for a Christian life: *All our works should be for the advantage of others.* In that every Christian has such abundance through faith, all his works—indeed his whole life!— are above and beyond such an abundance in order spontaneously and with good will to serve and be of benefit to his neighbor.

---

[1]Cf. Philippians 2:7: "...but made himself nothing, taking the form of a servant, being born in the likeness of men. And being found in human form,..."

[2]Cf. 1 Thessalonians 4:11; 2 Thessalonians 3:6-12.

[3]Cf. "Let the thief no longer steal, but rather let him labor, doing honest work with his own hands, so that he may have something to share with anyone in need" Ephesians 4:28.

[4]Cf. "We who are strong have an obligation to bear with the failings of the weak, and not to please ourselves" Romans 15:1.

[5]Cf. "By this it is evident who are the children of God, and who are the children of the devil: whoever does not practice righteousness is not of God, nor is the one who does not love his brother" 1 John 3:10;

Romans 8:16.
[6]Cf. Galatians 6:2.
[7]Cf. Galatians 5:6.

———————

1. Who do we live for besides God (*Galatians 6:9,10*)?

2. What is the Christian's position to others (*Luke 6:35* and *Hebrews 13:16*)?

3. Who is our example (*Philippians 2:7*)?

4. Compare *Romans 15:1, I John 3:10,* and *Galatians 6:2-5* and explain in your own words what is being said.

13

WORKING LIKE CHRIST

Paul makes note of Christ as an example of how we should serve others, saying:

"Have this mind among yourselves, which is yours in Christ Jesus, who, though he was in the form of God, did not count equality with God a thing to be grasped, but made himself nothing, taking the form of a servant, being born in the likeness of men. And being found in human form, he humbled himself by becoming obedient to the point of death" (Philippians 2:5-8).

This most beneficial statement by the Apostle has become confusing for us to understand because some, totally misunderstanding the expressions "form of God," "form of a servant," "fashion," and "likeness of men," have transferred them solely to the natures of Godhead and manhood. Paul's meaning is this: Christ was full of the form of God and abounded in all good things. Christ needed no works or sufferings to be justified and saved. All good things Christ had from the very beginning—but He did not become conceited because of them. Christ did not raise Himself above us and take to Himself power over us.

> **Christ needed no works or sufferings to be justified and saved**

Rightfully Christ could have done just that. On the contrary, He labored, worked, suffered, and died in order to be like all other people. In short, Christ was nothing other than a human being in fashion and in conduct—just as if He needed everything and had nothing.

Yet all this He did for our sakes. He did it to serve us. He did it that all His works in the form of a servant might become ours.

A Christian, like Christ *the* Christian's *head*,[1] having abundance through faith, should be content with this same form of God obtained by faith. He ought, however, to increase in this faith until it be perfected.

The faith of the Christian is, after all, his life. It is also a Christian's justification and salvation, preserving him and making him pleasing to God. The Christian's faith also bestows upon him all that Christ has, as I have said above, and as Paul affirms: "The life I now live in the flesh I live by faith in the Son of God" (Galatians

2:20).

Although a Christian is free from all works, he ought to empty himself of this liberty, take on himself the form of a servant, be made in the likeness of men, be found in fashion as a man, serve, help, and in every way act towards his neighbor as he sees that God through Christ has acted and is acting towards him. All this he should do freely, and with regard to nothing but the good pleasure of God. The Christian should think in this way:

"My God, without merit on my part, of His pure and free mercy, has given to me, an unworthy, condemned, and contemptible person, all the riches of justification and salvation in Christ. I no longer need anything, except faith to believe that this is so. For such a Father, then, who has overwhelmed me with these inestimable riches of His, why should I not freely, cheerfully, and with my whole heart, and from voluntary zeal, do all that I know will be pleasing to Him and acceptable in His sight? I will therefore give myself as a sort of Christ to my neighbor, as Christ has given Himself to me; and will do nothing in this life except what I see will be needful, advantageous, and wholesome for my neighbor, since by faith I abound in all good things in Christ."

In such a way, love and joy in the Lord flow from faith. From such a cheerful, willing, free spirit, a Christian is disposed to serve his neighbor voluntarily, without taking any account of gratefulness or ungratefulness, credit or fault, profit or loss.

The goal of such service is not to make people feel obligated toward the Christian. Such service does not distinguish between friends and enemies. Such service does not look for gratefulness or ungratefulness, but most freely and willingly it gives itself and its possessions, whether it loses them through ungratefulness, or gains goodwill.

The Christian's Father, in just the same way, distributes everything to everyone abundantly and freely. The sun of the Father *rises upon the just and the unjust.*[2] In the same way also the child of the Father does and endures nothing except from the free joy with which it delights through Christ in God, the Giver of such great gifts.[3]

You see, then, if we recognize those *great and precious gifts,*[4] as Peter says, which have been given to us, love is quickly diffused in our hearts through the Spirit. By love we are made free, joyful, all-powerful, active workers, victors over all our tribulations, servants to our neighbor, and, at the same time, lords of all things.

For those who do not recognize the good things given to them through Christ, however, Christ has indeed been born in vain. Such people live by works, and will never attain the taste and feeling of these great things.

Therefore just as our neighbor is in need, and needs our abundance, so too we, in the sight of God, were in need and had need of His mercy. As our heavenly Father has freely helped us in Christ, so ought we freely to help our neighbor with our body and works. Each Christian should become to another a sort of Christ. In this way we will be Christs to each other,

Each Christian should become to another a sort of Christ

and that same Christ will be in all of us—that is, we will truly be Christians.

[1]"And he is the head of the body, the church. He is the beginning, the firstborn from the dead, that in everything he might be preeminent" Colossians 1:18. Cf. Colossians 2:9-10.

[2]Cf. Matthew 5:45.

[3]"Every good gift and every perfect gift is from above, coming down from the Father of lights with whom there is no variation or shadow due to change" James 1:17.

[4]"His divine power has granted to us all things that pertain to life and godliness, through the knowledge of him who called us to his own glory and excellence, by which he has granted to us his precious and very great promises, so that through them you may become partakers of the divine nature..." 2 Peter 1:3-4.

---

1. Who was Jesus (*John 1:1*, *Colossians 2:9*, *Acts 2:36*, and *John 15:10*)?

2. What was the attitude of Jesus (*Matthew 11:29*, *John 13:5*, and *Matthew 20:28*)?

3. So what is our relationship to Him (*John 5:24* and *Romans 10:9*)?

4. What do Christians have in this world (*Romans 5:3* and *I Corinthians 15:57*)?

14

THE RICHES AND GLORY OF THE CHRISTIAN

Who then can comprehend the riches and glory of the Christian? The Christian can do all things, has all things, and needs nothing. The Christian is lord over sin, death, and hell. At the same time the Christian is an obedient and useful servant to all.

Unfortunately this is unknown throughout the world. It is neither preached nor desired. We don't know the meaning of our own name. We don't know why we *are* Christians and why we are *called* Christians.

We are certainly called to be Christians by Christ. He is not absent from us but dwells among us—provided, that is, that we believe in Him and are reciprocally and mutually Christs to one another, doing to our neighbor as Christ does to us.

Nowadays, however, we are taught by many to seek merits, rewards, and things that are already ours. We have made of Christ a taskmaster far more severe than Moses.

Mary, beyond all others, provides us with an example of such a faith. Like all other Jewish women, she was purified [after the birth of Christ] according to the law of Moses[1]—even though she was bound by no such law and had no need of purification. Mary submitted to the law voluntarily, however, and of free love, made herself just like the rest of women, that she might not offend or throw contempt on them.

She was not justified by doing this. Being already justified, she did it freely and gratuitously. In the same way our works ought to be done, not to be justified by them, but simply to do them freely and cheerfully for the sake of others.

St. Paul circumcised his disciple Timothy,[2] not because he needed circumcision for his justification, but that he might not offend or condemn those Jews who, weak in the faith, had not yet been able to comprehend the liberty of faith. On the other hand, when the Jews condemned liberty and urged that circumcision was necessary for justification, he resisted them, and would not allow Titus to be circumcised.[3] For as he would not offend or condemn any one's weakness in faith, but yielded for the time to their will, so, again, he would not have the liberty of faith offended or condemned by hardened selfjustifiers.

Paul took the middle road, sparing the weak for a time, and always resisting the hardened, that he might convert all to the liberty of faith. We ought to act using the same principle, receiving those who are weak in the faith,[4] but boldly resisting these hardened teachers of works, of whom we shall hereafter speak a little more.

Christ also, when His disciples were asked for the tribute money, asked of Peter whether the children of a king were not free from taxes.[5] Peter agreed that they were. Yet Jesus commanded Peter to go to the sea, saying, "However, not to give offense to them, go to the sea and cast a hook and take the first fish that comes up, and when you open its mouth you will find a shekel. Take that and give it to them for me and for yourself" (Matthew 17:27).

> *Paul took the middle road, sparing the weak for a time, and always resisting the hardened*

Such an example nicely demonstrates the point I am making. Here Christ calls Himself and His disciples free men and children of a king. As such they are in want of nothing. Still Christ voluntarily submits and pays the tax. As far as this work was necessary or useful to Christ for justification or salvation, so far also were all His other works or those of His disciples beneficial for their justification. They are really free and occur after justification. Such works are done only to serve others and give them an example.

This is the type of works which Paul taught.[6]

Christians should be *subject to principalities and powers* and *ready to do every good work*,[7] but not in order to be justified by these things. Christians are already justified by faith! Christians do such works, however, that in liberty of spirit they may in such a way be the servants of others and subject to powers, obeying their will out of gratuitous love.

Such, too, ought to have been the works of all colleges, monasteries, and priests. Each should have been doing the works of his own profession and station of life. Not in order to be justified by them, but in order to bring his own body into subjection as an example to others, who themselves also need to keep their bodies under control, and also in order to accommodate himself to the will of others, out of free love.

But we must always guard most carefully against any vain confidence or presumption of being justified, gaining merit, or being saved by these works. Faith alone does this, as I have so often said.

Any man possessing this knowledge may easily keep clear of danger among the innumerable commands and precepts of the pope, of bishops, of monasteries, of churches, of princes, and of magistrates, which some foolish pastors urge on us as being necessary for justification and salvation. They call them precepts of the Church, when they are not. The Christian freeman will speak in this way:

"I will fast, I will pray, I will do this or that which is commanded me by men, not as having any need of these things for justification or salvation, but that I may thus comply with the will of the pope, of the bishop, of such a community or such a magistrate, or of my neighbor as an example to him. For this cause I will do and suffer all things, just as Christ did and suffered much more for me. Although Christ did not need to do so on His own account, He made Himself for my sake under the law, when He was not under the law. And although tyrants may do me violence or wrong

Any Christian should be able to judge confidently and evaluate faithfully any work or law

in requiring obedience to these things, yet it will not hurt me to do them, so long as they are not done against God."

Considering all of these things, any Christian should be able to judge confidently and evaluate faithfully any work or law. He should also be able to distinguish between those pastors who are blind and inane and those who are true and good.

Any work done neither to subdue our flesh nor to serve our neighbor (provided such a work is not contrary to the will of God!) is neither a good nor Christian work! Nowadays few Christian colleges, seminaries, churches or churchly activities should be considered Christian. The same could be said for fasts and prayers to the saints. What is being sought in all of these things is already ours!

By participating in such things we hope to purge away our sins and attain salvation and in so doing, completely destroy Christian liberty! This is due simply to our ignorance of the Christian faith and its liberty.

Ignorance of the Christian faith and the destruction of Christian liberty is promoted by the teaching of many pastors. Such pastors stir up their people and urge them to be zealous for such things, praising them and causing them to become conceited when they purchase an indulgence. These same pastors, however, never preach faith.

Now if you truly want to pray, to fast, or to create an endowment fund for the church, do not do so in order to receive some sort of earthly or heavenly benefit. In doing so you offend your faith which alone is the source of everything you have.

Indeed it is the increase of faith, through work or suffering, which should always be your goal. Whatever you give, give freely without hope of reward. Give simply so that others may prosper and benefit from your goodness. In such a way you will be a truly good person and a Christian.

The good things which we have received from God should flow from one Christian to another

What good are your wealth and works over and above those needed to keep your flesh in subjugation? You have received abundantly through faith in which God has given you all things.

Here is a good rule of thumb concerning this topic: The good things which we have received from God should flow from one Christian to another and become common to all. In such a way each Christian can put on his neighbor[8] and therefore act towards him as if he himself were his neighbor.

Such good things flowed and continue to flow from Christ to us. He *put us on.* Christ acted for us as if He Himself were what we are.

Such good things flow from us to those who need them. This means that my faith and righteousness ought to be laid down before God as a covering and intercession for the sins of my neighbor. My neighbor's sins I am to take on myself. I am to work and serve in them just as if they were my own.

This is what Christ has done for us. This is true love and the genuine truth of Christian life, present only where there is true and genuine faith. Hence the Apostle Paul attributes to love this quality: *It seeks not its own way.*[9]

In conclusion then, it must be asserted that a Christian does not live in himself, but in Christ and in his neighbor. If a Christian does not live in such a way, he is no Christian.

A Christian lives in Christ by faith and in his neighbor by love. By faith he is carried upwards above himself to God, and by love he sinks back below himself to his neighbor, still always abiding in God and His love, as Christ says, "Truly, truly, I say to you, you will see heaven opened, and the angels of God ascending and descending on the Son of Man" (John 1:51).

This is about all there is to say, at this point, about Christian freedom. As you can tell, Christian freedom is truly spiritual freedom which frees our hearts from all sins, laws and commandments as Paul says, "The law is not laid down for the just" (1 Timothy 1:9). As far as heaven is above the earth, Christian freedom surpasses all other external liberties. May Christ grant us understanding and preservation of this liberty. Amen.

[1] Cf. Luke 2:22-24 and Leviticus 12.
[2] Cf. Acts 16:3.
[3] Cf. Galatians 2:3.
[4] Cf. Romans 14:1.
[5] Cf. Matthew 17:25.
[6] Cf. Romans 12:17.
[7] Cf. Titus 3:1.
[8] Cf. Philippians 2:7 and Colossians 3.
[9] Cf. 1 Corinthians 13:5.

---

1. So what can we do on this earth (*Philippians 4:11-13, Colossians 2:13-15,* and *Colossians 2:6-7*)?

2. How are we to be in our daily life (*I John 2:24* and *I Peter 2:12*)?

3. Yet to whom are we also subject (*Titus 3:1-8*)?

4. What about our treatment of others (*John 13:35* and *I Peter 1:22*)?

5. Of what must we be aware (*I John 4:1-6*)?

6. Summarize the Christian life from *Galatians 5:6, I John 4:16,* and *Galatians 2:20.*

7. Whose help do Christians need (*John 8:34-36*)?

15

THE ABUSE OF CHRISTIAN FREEDOM

Finally, a few words must be written for those who will have a hard time understanding what I have written and so distort it. A word or two must be added so that such people may also understand.

Certainly there are many people who, when they hear about this liberty of faith, immediately take advantage of this liberty in the wrong way. They think that everything is now lawful. They demonstrate that they are free from the law and truly Christians by declaring that rituals, traditions and human laws are simply contemptible and reprehensible.

Such people seem to believe that their Christianity is based upon their refusal to fast, their eating of meat in front of those who are fasting, and their omitting of customary prayers. Such people scoff at the regulations of men, but completely disregard everything else that has to do with Christianity.

In contrast, there are those who strictly oppose such people, and who seek their salvation solely on the basis of their observance of and reverence for rituals. Such observance and reverence is so intense it frequently appears as if they would be saved merely because they fast on certain days, or abstain from eating meat, or make formal prayers. Such people talk loudly about the precepts of the Church and of the Church Fathers, and care nothing for those things which indicate genuine faith.

Both of these groups are obviously heading down the wrong road. Both neglect matters which are of weight and necessary for salvation while at the same time they contend noisily about things that are neither significant nor necessary. The Apostle Paul teaches us to take the middle road, condemning both extremes and saying, "Let not the one that eats despise the one that abstains, and let not the one who abstains pass judgment on the one who eats" (Romans 14:3)! Here the Apostle indicts those who disregard and complain about rituals simply on the basis of their

> **Those who cling to the observance of such rituals are not to judge those who do not**

contempt for them—not because of any religious feeling. Such rituals the Apostle teaches the Romans not to despise since such "knowledge puffs up." [1]

In the same way, Paul teaches that those who cling to the observance of such rituals are not to judge those who do not. When such judgment takes place, neither group shows a love to the other which edifies.

In this matter we must listen to the Word of God, which teaches us neither to *go to the right hand or to the left*,[2] but to follow those right precepts of the Lord which cause the heart to rejoice.[3] A man is not righteous because he serves and is devoted to works and rituals. Neither is a man deemed righteous because he neglects or despises them.

Faith in Christ does not set us free from works. Faith sets us free from a belief in works, that is, from a foolish presumption to seek our justification through works. Faith redeems our consciences, makes them upright, and preserves them. By faith we recognize the truth that justification does not depend upon our works.

However, good works should not and cannot be lacking—just as we cannot exist without food and drink and all the functions of our bodies. Still our justification is not based on works, but on faith.

Just because our justification is based on faith, however, our works should not be despised or neglected. In this world we are compelled by the needs of this bodily life, but they do not justify us. "My kingdom is not *of* this world,"[4] says Christ. He does not say, "My kingdom is not here, that is, *in* this world." Paul, too, says, "Though we walk in the flesh, we are not waging war according to the flesh" (2 Corinthians 10:3), and "The life I now live in the flesh I live by faith in the Son of God" (Galatians 2:20). Our actions, life, and being, in works and rituals, are done from the necessities of this life, and with the motive of governing our bodies. Yet we are not justified by these things, but by the faith of the Son of God.

> **Our works should not be despised or neglected just because our justification is based on faith**

The Christian must take the middle path between these two groups of people. He may meet with hardened and obstinate ritualists, who, like deaf adders, refuse to listen to the truth of liberty.[5] Such people cry out, enjoin, and urge on us their rituals—as if they could justify us without faith. Such were the Jews of old, who would not understand, that they might act well.

These men we must resist. We must do just the contrary to what they do. We must be bold to offend them so that they do not, by this impious notion of theirs, deceive many others along with themselves. Before the eyes of these men it is proper to eat meat, to break fasts, and to do on behalf of the freedom of faith things which they hold to be the greatest sins. We must say of them, "Let them alone; they are blind guides" (Matthew 15:14). In this way Paul also would not have Titus circumcised,[6] though these men urged it. In the same way Christ defended the Apostles, who had plucked heads of grain on the Sabbath day.[7]

We may also meet simple minded and unknowing people, *weak*[8] in faith (as the Apostle calls them), who are as yet unable to comprehend the freedom of faith, even if they were willing to do so.[9] These we must spare so that they will not be offended. We must bear with their infirmity, till they shall be more fully instructed.

These people do not act in such a way from hardened malice, but only from weakness of faith. In order to avoid giving them offence, we must keep fasts and do other things which they consider necessary. This is required of us by love, which injures no one, but serves all men. It is not the fault of these people that they are weak, but that of their pastors,

> **We should fight vigorously against the wolves on behalf of the sheep, but not fight against the sheep**

who by the snares and weapons of their own traditions have brought them into bondage and wounded their souls.

They ought to have been set free and healed by the teaching of faith and liberty. The Apostle therefore says, "If food makes my brother stumble, I will never eat meat" (1 Corinthians 8:13).[10] Again he says "I know, and am persuaded in the Lord Jesus, that nothing is unclean in itself, but it is unclean for anyone who thinks it unclean...It is wrong for anyone to make another stumble by what he eats" (Romans 14:14,20).

We should boldly resist those teachers of tradition. And even though the regulations of the popes (by which the people of God are assaulted) deserve sharp reproof, we must spare those among us who are timid, who are held captive by the laws of those impious tyrants, till they are set free.

We should fight vigorously against the wolves on behalf of the sheep, but not fight against the sheep. And this you may do by denouncing laws and lawgivers, and yet at the same time, observing the same laws with the weak, lest they be offended.

This you should do until they themselves recognize the tyranny, and understand their own liberty. If you wish to use your liberty, do it secretly, as Paul says, "That faith you have, keep between yourself and God" (Romans 14:22).

Be careful not to use it in the presence of the weak. In the presence of tyrants and the obstinate however, use your liberty to spite them. Use your liberty yourself with the utmost obstinance, that they too may understand that they are tyrants, their laws are useless for justification, and that they have no right to establish such laws.

[1]Cf. 1 Corinthians 8:1.

[2]Deuteronomy 28:14.

[3]Cf. Psalm 19:8.

[4]Cf. John 18:36

[5]Cf. Psalm 58:4.

[6]Cf. Galatians 2:3.

[7]Cf. Matthew 12:1-8.

[8]Cf. 1 Corinthians 9:22.

[9]Cf. Romans 14:1.

[10]Cf. Romans 14:21.

1. Do Christians scoff at all regulations (*Galatians 5:13, I Corinthians 10:27-33, Matthew 5:20*, and *I Corinthians 8:1*)?

2. So what does faith do for Christians in their daily lives (*Titus 3:5, Romans 3:24*, and *Romans 11:6*)?

3. How about good deeds (*I Timothy 6:16, James 2:17,18*, and *I Peter 2:12*)?

4. Explain *II Thessalonians 2:9-12,15*.

16

A PROPER UNDERSTANDING OF RITUALS

Let's be honest. We cannot live in this world without works and rituals. The hot and inexperienced period of youth needs restraining and protection by such things.

Since every one is obligated to keep his own body under control by attention to these things, the minister of Christ must be prudent and faithful in so directing and teaching the people of Christ in all these matters. He should do this so that no root of bitterness may spring up among them, and many be defiled, as Paul warned the Hebrews.[1]

In other words, they must be properly instructed so

that they may not lose the faith, and begin to be defiled by a belief in works as the means of justification. This can happen easily, and defile many, unless faith be constantly taught along with works.

It is impossible to avoid this evil when faith is passed over in silence and only the ordinances of men are taught,

> **It is impossible to avoid this evil when faith is passed over in silence and only the ordinances of man are taught**

as has been done up until now by the pestilent, impious, and soul-destroying traditions of our popes and opinions of our theologians. An infinite number of souls have been drawn down to hell by these snares, so that you may recognize the work of the antichrist.

In brief, as poverty is endangered when it is among riches, honesty among business, humility among honors, abstinence among feasting, and purity among pleasures, so is justification by faith endangered among rituals. Solomon says, "Can a man take fire in his bosom, and his clothes not be burned?" (Proverbs 6:27).

And yet as we must live among riches, business, honors, pleasures, and feasts, so must we live among rituals, that is among perils. Just as infant boys have the greatest need of being cherished in the bosoms and by the care of girls, that they may not die, and yet, when they are grown, there is peril to their salvation in living among girls, so inexperienced and fervid young men require to be kept in and restrained by the barriers of rituals, even were they of iron, lest their weak minds should rush headlong into vice.

And yet it would be death to them to persevere in believing that they can be justified by these things. They must rather be taught that they have been thus imprisoned, not with the purpose of their being justified or gaining merit in this way, but in order that they might avoid wrong-doing, and be more easily instructed in that righteousness which is by faith, a thing which the headlong character of youth would not bear unless it were put under restraint.

Hence in the Christian life rituals are to be looked upon as builders and workmen look upon those preparations for building or working which are not made with any view of being permanent or anything in themselves, but only because without them there could be no building and no work. When the structure is completed, they are laid aside.

Here you see that we do not despise these preparations, but set the highest value on them. It is a belief in them we despise, because no one thinks that they constitute a real and permanent structure.

If any one were so manifestly out of his senses as to have no other object in life than that of setting up these preparations with all possible expense, diligence, and perseverance, while he never thought of the structure itself, but pleased himself and made his boast of these useless preparations and props, should we not all pity his madness and think, that at the cost thus thrown away, some great building might

> **We do not despise these preparations... it is a belief in them we despise**

have been raised?

Thus, too, we do not despise works and rituals—nay, we set the highest value on them. But we despise the belief in works, which no one should consider to constitute true righteousness, as do those hypocrites who employ and throw away their whole life in the pursuit of works, and yet never attain to that for the sake of which the works are done. As the Apostle says, they are "ever learning and never able to come to the knowledge of the truth" (2 Timothy 3:7). They appear to wish to build, they make preparations, and yet they never do build. In this way they continue in a show of godliness, but never attain to its power.[2]

Meanwhile they please themselves with this zealous pursuit, and even dare to judge all others, whom they do not see adorned with such a glittering display of works. If such people had been endowed with faith, they might have done great things for their own and others' salvation, at the same cost which they now waste in abuse of the gifts of God.

But since human nature and natural reason, as they call it, are naturally superstitious, and quick to believe that justification can be attained by any laws or works proposed to them, and since nature is also exercised and confirmed in the same view by the practice of all earthly lawgivers, she can never of her own power free herself from this bondage to works, and come to a recognition of the freedom of faith.

We pray then that God will teach us,[3] that is, make us always ready to learn of Him; and will Himself, as He has promised, write His law in our hearts. Otherwise there is no hope for us.

For unless He himself teaches us inwardly this wisdom hidden in a mystery,[4] nature cannot but condemn it and consider it to be nonsense. She takes offence at it, and it seems foolish to her, just as we see that it happened long ago in the case of the prophets and Apostles, and just as blind and impious pontiffs, with their flatterers, do now in my case and that of those who are like me. *May God be gracious to us..., and make His face to shine upon us, that we may know His way on earth and His saving power among all nations,*[5] who is blessed for evermore. Amen.

---

[1]"See to it that no one fails to obtain the grace of God; that no "root of bitterness" springs up and causes trouble, and by it many become defiled;" Hebrews 12:15.

[2]Cf. 2 Timothy 3:5.

[3]Cf. John 6:45.

[4]Cf. 1 Corinthians 2:7.

[5]Cf. Psalm 67:1-2.

═══════════════

1. What can happen to Christians (*II Timothy 4:3-5*)?

2. What is the warning in *Hebrews 12:15*?

3. What is the work of the antichrist (*I Thessalonians 2:9-17*)?

4. How can Christians be taught properly (*John 6:45*)?

AFTERWORD

The genesis of this work was my frustration at not being able to find a book which would simply and clearly lay out for the average Christian the 'every-day' of Christian life. My search for such a work eventually led me to the relatively unknown work of Martin Luther, *On Christian Freedom* (*De libertate christiana*). English editions of this classic, however, turned out to be too difficult to read. The problem lay in translation. The scholarly had to be reshaped for the 'everyman'. Luther's German had to be translated into Hemingway's English. The semi-colon had to be all but banished and the paragraph-long sentence disappear.

This work, then, began simply as a revision of the translation of R. S. Grignon, (*Christian Freedom*, The FiveFoot Shelf of Books, The Harvard Classics, Vol. 36, New York: P. F. Collier & Son, 1910, pp. 35-97) which is in the public domain. Initially it was thought that with just a little effort, this translation could be republished as it is for the benefit of all. The woodeness of the translation, however, made it unsuitable for modern minds. The translation of the American Edition of Luther's Works (Volume 31) by W.A. Lambert, revised by Harold J. Grimm was also consulted. In this edition, however, readability was sacrificed on the altar of accuracy. I was therefore driven back to the critical edition of both the original Latin and German editions of 1520 available in the recently published *Studienausgabe* of Luther's writings (Vol. 2, pp. 260-309, Berlin: Evangelische Verlagsanstalt, 1982) and faced with more work than originally determined necessary (or desired!). The end result is a work which is not so wooden, not so accurate (unfortunately!), but, I hope, very readable!

The chapter headings in the work were added for clarity. The use of italics was employed to note where a) Luther cites sections of the Scripture but does not acknowledge that he is doing so, and b) where its use would help to add clarity to Luther's argument. Bible citations were standardized using the new English Standard Version (Wheaton: Crossway Bibles, 2001).

Here I must thank Scott Krieger for reformatting the entire text, creating the chapter divisions and titles, and in general, going over the work again and again with a fine tooth comb. The readability of this work in general is due to his efforts.

For its shortcomings, of which there are many, I alone take responsibility. Doubtless there are many others who, having wrestled with this text, could have fared much better. It is hoped, however, that in simply providing a somewhat updated edition of this work, it will once again enjoy the popularity it so richly deserves, and be of great benefit to all who read it.

Paul Strawn, Spring Lake Park, Minnesota
August 2003

Afterword
to 2nd Edition

The popularity of the 1st edition of this work has necessitated a second updated and expanded edition. To the original work has been added study questions prepared by Rev. Jack Baumgarn of St. Francis, Minnesota, and an index of Biblical References. Minor corrections to the text have also been made and while, regrettably, it remains somewhat awkward, the overall readability has improved. Once again my thanks to Scott Krieger for his tireless efforts in the production of this text.

Paul Strawn, Spring Lake Park, Minnesota
June 2006

BIBLICAL REFERENCES

Psalms (cont.)		Matthew (cont.)	
145:19	42	*5:20*	91
Proverbs		*5:45*	74,75
6:27	94	*7:15*	62,64
Song of Solomon		*7:15-20*	60
2:16	31	*7:18*	57
Isaiah		*7:20*	59
2:3	33	*9:13*	19
4:6	24	*11:7-10*	64
10:22-23	18	*11:29*	75
53:4	33	*12:1-8*	88,90
53:6	33	*12:33*	58
Lamentations		*13:52*	63,64
5:7-9	46	*15:14*	59,60,88
Hosea		*17:25*	79,84
2:19	31	*17:27*	79
2:20	31	*20:28*	75
6:6	19	*25:35*	60
13:9	22	*25:36*	60
Amos		*28:18*	36,37
8:11	15,19	Mark	
Micah		*14:36*	41,43
3:8	43	*16:16*	18
Matthew		Luke	
3:1	65	*1:26-35*	35,36
3:2	63,65	*1:35*	37
3:6	65	*2:22-24*	78,84
3:8-10	65	*3:7-10*	65
4:4	15	*3:18*	65
5:18	22,24	*6:35*	70

Luke (cont.)		Acts	
6:39	59,60	2:22-24	65
12:22	19	2:36	75
John		2:36-39	65
1:1	75	4:33	43
1:12	24	15:5-11	64
1:16	20	15:10	61,64
1:51	83	16:3	78,84
4:13-14	11	**Romans**	
4:14	9	1:1-4	16,19
5:24	75	1:17	16
6:27	18	3:10-12	17
6:29	18	3:21-24	33
6:45	96,97	3:23	16
8:31-32	11,33	3:24	91
8:32	43	3:28	20
8:34-36	84	4:2-3	28,32,33
8:36	15	4:23-5:5	33
11:25	15	5:1	52
13:5	75	5:3	75
13:35	84	5:1-5	24
14:26	36,37	5:15-19	48
15:7	43	5:8	48
15:5-8	33	6:13	54
15:10	75	7:7	24
15:16	33	7:12-14	24
17	37	7:22-23	51
18:36	37,87,90	7:24-25	24
18:38	36	7:25	52
20:31	24	8:1-4	20

Romans (cont.)		1st Corinthians	
8:5-8	43	1:30	48
8:12-14	20	2:7	97
8:15	43	2:14	60
8:16	68,70	3:22-23	40
8:23	50,57	4:1	46
8:28	40,41,43	6:19	19
8:35-37	48	8:1	82,90,91
10:4	16	8:8	19
10:9	16,75	8:13	89
10:9-10	19	9:25	52
10:10	17,18	9:27	51
10:17	64	9:19	10,11
11:6	64,91	9:19-23	11
11:32	23,27,32	9:22	89,90
12:2	33	10:27-33	91
12:17	79,84	12:3	60
13:8	10	13:4-7	11
13:8-10	11	13:5	84,85
13:14	33	15:57	31,48,75
14:1	79,84,89,90	2nd Corinthians	
14:3	86	3:17	43
14:7-8	67	4:16	11
14:14	89	5:8	19
14:17	19	5:18	20
14:20	89	5:18-19	33
14:21	89,90	10:3	88
14:22	90	12:7-10	43
15:1	68,69,70	12:8-9	40,43
15:4	20,24		

Galatians		Ephesians (cont.)	
2:3	78,84,88,90	6:14	33
2:16	60	6:18	43
2:20	72,73,84,88	**Philippians**	
3:22-25	20	1:11	33
3:24	24	1:20-21	33
4:4	10,11	2:1-4	69
4:6	43	2:5-8	71
4:8-11	64	2:6	10,11
5:6	60,68,70,84	2:7	10,11,68,69
5:13	60		70,82,84
5:13-26	11	3:8-9	33
5:17	11	3:9	24
5:19-21	54	3:12	60
5:22-26	60	3:13-14	52
5:24	51	4:11-13	84
6:2	68,70	4:13	33
6:2-5	70	**Colossians**	
6:9-10	70	1:18	37,72,73
Ephesians		2:6-7	84
1:22	37	2:9	75
2:8-10	52	2:9-10	75
2:12	11	2:13-15	84
2:13	11	2:20-23	65
2:19-22	11	3	82,84
2:28-32	33	3:1-4	33
4:28	68,69	3:12-14	33
5:26-27	30,32	**1st Thessalonians**	
5:32	28,32	4:11	68,69
6:7	60		

2nd Thessalonians		Hebrews	
2:9-12	91	1	36,37
2:9-17	97	4:14-5:10	37
2:15	91	4:16	48
3:6-12	68,69	7	36,37
1st Timothy		7:23-25	36,37
1:9	26,84	9:11-14	37
1:15-17	48	10:19-22	48
4:1-16	48	11:6	58
4:7-8	19	12:1	54
5:24-25	59,60	12:15	93,97
6:8	52	13:16	70
6:11	33	James	
6:16	91	1:2-4	43
2nd Timothy		1:17	74,75
1:3	60	2:10	24
2:12	43	2:17-18	91
3:5	59,96,97	2:19	48
3:7	59,96	4:7	54
3:13	59,60	1st Peter	
3:16-17	43	1:22	84
4:2-5	48	2:2	19
4:3-5	97	2:5-10	43
Titus		2:9	39,43,60
1:7-9	48	2:12	84,91
3:1	80,84	2:24	33
3:1-8	84	3:22	36,37
3:5	52,60,64,91	5:10	17,19
4:1-5	65		

2ⁿᵈ Peter

1:3-4	74,75
3:18	52

1ˢᵗ John

1:8	24
2:2	37
2:24	84
3:10	68,69,70
3:16	52
4:1-6	84
4:16	84
5:13	24

Jude

24-25	65

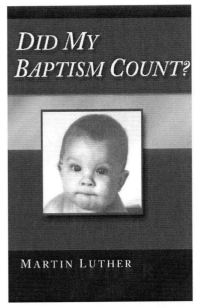

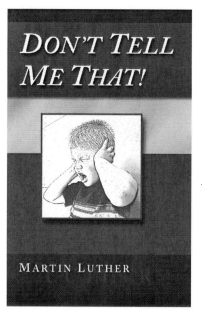